First World War
and Army of Occupation
War Diary
France, Belgium and Germany

66 DIVISION
Divisional Troops
Royal Army Service Corps
Divisional Train (541, 542, 543, 544 Companies A.S.C.)
19 September 1915 - 3 November 1915

WO95/3133/1

The Naval & Military Press Ltd
www.nmarchive.com
Published in association with The National Archives

Published by

The Naval & Military Press Ltd

Unit 10 Ridgewood Industrial Park,

Uckfield, East Sussex,

TN22 5QE England

Tel: +44 (0) 1825 749494

www.naval-military-press.com

www.nmarchive.com

This diary has been reprinted in facsimile from the original. Any imperfections are inevitably reproduced and the quality may fall short of modern type and cartographic standards.

© **Crown Copyright**
Images reproduced by permission of The National Archives, London, England, 2015.

Contents

Document type	Place/Title	Date From	Date To
Heading	66th Division 66th (E.L) Divl Train ASC Mar 1917-June 1919 1915 Sept 1916 Feb And 1917 Mar To 1919 June 541-544 Coys ASC		
Heading	WO95/3133/1		
Heading	66 Division Troops 66 Div Train and 541 to 544 Coy ASC 1915 Sep-1916 Feb		
War Diary	Crowborough	01/10/1915	11/10/1915
War Diary	Maidstone	12/10/1915	12/10/1915
War Diary	Crowborough	14/10/1915	14/10/1915
War Diary	Tunbridge Wells	17/10/1915	18/10/1915
War Diary	Crowborough	18/10/1915	20/10/1915
War Diary	Maidstone	20/10/1915	20/10/1915
War Diary	Tunbridge Wells	21/10/1915	21/10/1915
War Diary	Crowborough	21/10/1915	21/10/1915
War Diary	Tunbridge Wells	22/10/1915	22/10/1915
War Diary	Crowborough	23/10/1915	23/10/1915
War Diary	Maidstone	25/10/1915	25/10/1915
War Diary	Tonbridge	26/10/1915	29/10/1915
War Diary	Crowborough	28/10/1915	28/10/1915
War Diary	Tunbridge Wells	29/10/1915	29/10/1915
War Diary	Crowborough	29/10/1915	02/11/1915
War Diary	East Grinstead	02/11/1915	02/11/1915
War Diary	Crowborough	02/11/1915	03/11/1915
War Diary	Tunbridge Wells	03/11/1915	03/11/1915
War Diary	East Grinstead	05/11/1915	05/11/1915
War Diary	Crowborough	06/11/1915	06/11/1915
War Diary	East Grinstead	09/11/1915	09/11/1915
War Diary	Crowborough	15/11/1915	15/11/1915
War Diary	East Grinstead	15/11/1915	23/11/1915
War Diary	Crowborough	20/11/1915	20/11/1915
War Diary	East Grinstead	23/11/1915	23/11/1915
War Diary	Crowborough	00/00/1917	00/00/1917
War Diary	Hartfield	20/01/1916	20/01/1916
War Diary	Crowborough	16/02/1916	16/02/1916
War Diary	Hartfield	20/01/1916	20/01/1916
War Diary	Crowborough	16/02/1916	16/02/1916
Miscellaneous	Monthly Statement Rendered in Connection With War Diaries	02/09/1915	02/09/1915
War Diary	Crowborough	04/10/1915	14/10/1915
War Diary	E. Grinstead	14/10/1915	31/12/1915
War Diary	Crowborough	04/10/1915	14/10/1915
War Diary	E. Grinstead	14/10/1915	16/02/1916
Miscellaneous	Monthly Statement in Connection With War Diaries	04/09/1915	04/09/1915
War Diary	E. Grinstead	16/02/1916	16/02/1916
War Diary	Crowborough	14/10/1915	21/10/1915
War Diary	Tunbridge Wells	29/10/1915	03/11/1915
War Diary	Crowborough	14/10/1915	21/10/1915
War Diary	Tunbridge Wells	29/10/1915	16/12/1915
Miscellaneous	War Diary Statement	01/09/1915	01/09/1915
War Diary	Peas Portage Camp	21/09/1915	21/09/1915

War Diary	East Grinstead	21/09/1915	22/09/1915
War Diary	Tunbridge	22/09/1915	23/09/1915
War Diary	Maidstone	25/09/1915	20/10/1915
War Diary	Tunbridge Wells	21/10/1915	21/10/1915
War Diary	Maidstone	24/10/1915	24/10/1915
War Diary	Crowborough	02/11/1915	20/11/1915
War Diary	Maidstone	20/10/1915	20/10/1915
War Diary	Tunbridge Wells	21/10/1915	21/10/1915
War Diary	Maidstone	24/10/1915	24/10/1915
War Diary	Crowborough	20/01/1916	29/02/1916
Miscellaneous	544 Coy ASC From Dec 1915 War Diary For September 1915		
War Diary	Crowborough	26/02/1916	29/02/1916
Miscellaneous	Statement		
War Diary	Crowborough	06/10/1915	01/03/1916
War Diary	Hartfield	20/01/1916	20/01/1916
War Diary	Crowborough	00/12/1915	00/12/1915
Heading	66 Division Senior Supply Officer 1915 Sep-1915 Dec		
Miscellaneous	Monthly Statement Rendered in Connection With War Diaries For August 1915	06/09/1915	06/09/1915
War Diary	Maidstone	19/09/1915	19/09/1915
War Diary	Tonbridge	19/09/1915	19/09/1915
War Diary	Crowborough	21/09/1915	25/09/1915
War Diary	Peas Pottage	21/09/1915	23/09/1915
War Diary	East Grinstead	21/09/1915	21/09/1915
War Diary	Tonbridge	22/09/1915	22/09/1915
War Diary	Maidstone	23/09/1915	23/09/1915
War Diary	Worthing	24/09/1915	24/09/1915
War Diary	Crowborough	27/09/1915	27/09/1915
War Diary	Maresfield Park	28/09/1915	28/09/1915
War Diary	Crowborough	21/09/1915	21/09/1915
War Diary	Pens Pottage	22/09/1915	22/09/1915
War Diary	East Grinstead	23/09/1915	23/09/1915
War Diary	Tonbridge	24/09/1915	24/09/1915
War Diary	Maidstone	25/09/1915	25/09/1915
War Diary	Crowborough	02/10/1915	02/10/1915
War Diary	Maidstone	19/09/1915	19/09/1915
War Diary	Tonbridge	19/09/1915	19/09/1915
War Diary	Crowborough	21/09/1915	25/09/1915
War Diary	Peas Pottage	21/09/1915	23/09/1915
War Diary	East Grinstead	21/09/1915	21/09/1915
War Diary	Tonbridge	21/09/1915	21/09/1915
War Diary	Maidstone	23/09/1915	23/09/1915
War Diary	Worthing	24/09/1915	24/09/1915
War Diary	Crowborough	27/09/1915	27/09/1915
War Diary	Maresfield Park	28/09/1915	28/09/1915
War Diary	Maidstone	19/09/1915	19/09/1915
War Diary	Tonbridge	19/09/1915	19/09/1915
War Diary	East Grinstead	21/09/1915	21/09/1915
War Diary	Tonbridge	22/09/1915	22/09/1915
War Diary	Maidstone	23/09/1915	23/09/1915
War Diary	Worthing	24/09/1915	24/09/1915
War Diary	Crowborough	21/09/1915	21/09/1915
War Diary	Peas Pottage	22/09/1915	22/09/1915
War Diary	East Grinstead	23/09/1915	23/09/1915
War Diary	Tonbridge	24/09/1915	24/09/1915

War Diary	Maidstone	25/09/1915	25/09/1915
War Diary	Crowborough	02/10/1915	02/10/1915
War Diary	Crowborough	27/09/1915	27/09/1915
War Diary	Maresfield Pare	28/09/1915	28/09/1915
War Diary	Maidstone	19/09/1915	19/09/1915
War Diary	Tonbridge	19/09/1915	19/09/1915
War Diary	East Grinstead	21/09/1915	21/09/1915
War Diary	Tonbridge	22/09/1915	22/09/1915
War Diary	Maidstone	23/09/1915	23/09/1915
War Diary	Worthing	24/09/1915	24/09/1915
War Diary	Crowborough	01/10/1915	01/10/1915
War Diary	Maidstone	01/10/1915	12/10/1915
War Diary	Tunbridge Wells	17/10/1915	18/10/1915
War Diary	Crowborough	27/09/1915	27/09/1915
War Diary	Maresfield Pare	28/09/1915	28/09/1915
War Diary	Tunbridge Wells	22/10/1915	22/10/1915
War Diary	Maidstone	25/10/1915	25/10/1915
War Diary	Tonbridge	26/10/1915	29/10/1915
War Diary	Crowborough	01/10/1915	01/10/1915
War Diary	Maidstone	01/10/1915	12/10/1915
War Diary	Tunbridge Wells	17/10/1915	18/10/1915
War Diary	East Grinstead	02/11/1915	02/11/1915
War Diary	Crowborough	02/11/1915	03/11/1915
War Diary	Tunbridge Wells	03/11/1915	03/11/1915
War Diary	Tunbridge Wells	22/10/1915	22/10/1915
War Diary	Maidstone	25/10/1915	25/10/1915
War Diary	Tonbridge	26/10/1915	29/10/1915
War Diary	East Grinstead	04/12/1915	04/12/1915
War Diary	Crowborough	04/12/1915	04/12/1915
War Diary	St Leonards.Hastings	05/12/1915	05/12/1915
War Diary	East Grinstead	08/12/1915	08/12/1915
War Diary	Crowborough	09/12/1915	13/12/1915
War Diary	East Grinstead	02/11/1915	02/11/1915
War Diary	Crowborough	02/11/1915	03/11/1915
War Diary	Tunbridge Wells	03/11/1915	03/11/1915

66TH DIVISION

66TH (E.L) DIVL TRAIN ASC.

MAR 1917-~~MAY 1919~~

JUNE 1919

1915 Sept - 1916 FEB
AND
1917 MAR to 1919 JUNE

541 - 544 Coys
ASC

WO 95/31331

66 DIVISION TROOPS

66 DIV TRAIN
AND
541 TO 544 COY ASC

1915 SEP — 1916 FEB

3019

Army Form C. 2118.

WAR DIARY
or
INTELLIGENCE SUMMARY.
(Erase heading not required.)

Instructions regarding War Diaries and Intelligence Summaries are contained in F.S. Regs., Part II. And the Staff Manual respectively. Title pages will be prepared in manuscript.

Hour, Date, Place	Summary of Events and Information	Remarks and references to Appendices
10.30 am. 1st October 1915. CROWBOROUGH.	A.D.S.T. Central Force inspected Divisional Supply Office at the Limes and proceeded to Supply Sepot at Crowborough Goods Station and Inspected books etc.	
2. 0 pm. 1st October 1915 MAIDSTONE.	Inspection by A.D.S.T. Central Force of Supply Depot, Staff and Books.	
4th October 1915. CROWBOROUGH.	Sent a Convoy to Peas Pottage, consisting of 11 wagons, 4 Riding horses and 22 Heavy Draught Horses.	
6.10.15. CROWBOROUGH.	Convoy to Pease Pottage returnung 9.10.15.	
11.10.15. CROWBOROUGH.	Convoy to Pease Pottage returning 13.10.15.	
4.0 pm. 12.10.15. MAIDSTONE.	Supply Depot 198th Infantry Brigade moved from Agricultural Hall to Monkton Drill Hall. No. 1 Coy.	
10.0 am. 14.10.15 CROWBOROUGH.	Removed from Crowborough to East Grinstead with 3 Officers 98 N.C.O's and men 15 wagons and 2 carts, 11 Riding Horses and 33 Heavy Draught Horses.	
10.0 am. 17th October 1915 TUNBRIDGE WELLS.	Supply Details 197th Infantry Brigade proceeded to TUNBRIDGE WELLS and took over Supply Duties. Depot handed over by O i/c Supplies 200th Infantry Brigade.	
10.0 am. 18.10.15. TUNBRIDGE WELLS.	First issue made from Tunbridge Wells Depot to 197th Infantry Brigade.	
18.10.15. CROWBOROUGH.	Convoy to Tunbridge Wells with Stores etc for 197th Infantry Brigade.	
19.10.15. CROWBOROUGH	Ditto. Ditto. Ditto.	
20.10.15. CROWBOROUGH	Ditto. Ditto. Ditto.	

Army Form C. 2118.

WAR DIARY
or
INTELLIGENCE SUMMARY.
(Erase heading not required.)

Instructions regarding War Diaries and Intelligence Summaries are contained in F. S. Regs., Part II. and the Staff Manual respectively. Title pages will be prepared in manuscript.

Hour, Date, Place	Summary of Events and Information	Remarks and references to Appendices
11.0 am. 20.10.15 MAIDSTONE.	No. 3 Coy. Horse Transport left Maidstone for Tunbridge Wells arriving 6.30.pm.	
8.30.am.21.10.15. TUNBRIDGE WELLS.	No. 3 Coy. Horse Transport left Tunbridge Wells for Crowborough arriving 1.0.pm. No. 2 Coy.	
7.0 am. 21.10.15.CROWBOROUGH.	We left Crowborough Camp for New Quarters at Tunbridge Wells by Route March - arrived at New Quarters (10 St. James Road Coy. Office) at 11.0 proceeded to unload Kits, Stores etc., N.C.O's & men billeted in empty houses. Complete issues made to Units of Middlesex Infantry Brigade en route from Falmer Camp to Sevenoaks.	
4.0 pm. 22.10.15. TUNBRIDGE WELLS.	Convoy to Burham, Nr. Maidstone, returning 26.10.15.	
23.10.15. CROWBOROUGH	No. 3 Coy. Supply Section left Maidstone for Crowborough arriving 7.30 pm.	
3.30 pm. 25.10.15.MAIDSTONE.	Supply Depot, Monkton Drill Hall handed over to 57th (West Lancs) Division Supply Details proceed to Crowborough	
10.0 am. 25.10.15.MAIDSTONE.	Supplies issued to advance parties of Battalions of 198th Infantry Brigade proceeding from BURHAM CAMP tp CROWBOROUGH by Officer i/c Supplies 197th Infantry Brigade TUNBRIDGE WELLS.	
26.10.15 & 29.10.15. TONBRIDGE.	Convoy to Burham Nr. Maidstone returning 31.10.15.	
28.10.15. CROWBOROUGH	Convoy left for Burham Camp to bring Stores etc to Crowborough. The night was spent at Burham Camp - the night of the 30th at Tonbridge Convoy returned to Tunbridge Wells on Sunday 31st inst, at 11.0 am and the wagons were taken on to Crowborough by No. 3 Coy. A.S.C.	
7.0 am. 29.10.15. TUNBRIDGE WELLS.		
October. CROWBOROUGH.	Farriers have attended an advanced in course in Cold Shoeing at Bermondsey.	
October. CROWBOROUGH.	2 N.C.O's attending a course of Musketry at BISLEY.	

Lt-Colonel,
Commdg. 68th (East Lancs.) Div. Train

Army Form C. 2118.

WAR DIARY
or
~~INTELLIGENCE SUMMARY~~
(Erase heading not required.)

Instructions regarding War Diaries and Intelligence Summaries are contained in F. S. Regs., Part II. and the Staff Manual respectively. Title pages will be prepared in manuscript.

Hour, Date, Place	Summary of Events and Information	Remarks and references to Appendices
CROWBOROUGH. 2.11.15. 10.45 am.	Major General F.H.B. Landon C.B. inspected No. 3 Company in Column of Route on the Maresfield Raod 1 mile from Camp. Harness (fitting of) and condition of horses were criticised. Efforts are now being made to remedy defects complained of.	
EAST GRINSTEAD. 2.11.15. 3.30 pm.	Inspection of Horses and Wagons by Chief Inspector Q.M.G. Services.	
EAST GRINSTEAD. 2.11.15. 5.0 pm.	Supply Depot EAST GRINSTEAD inspected by the Chief Inspector of Q.M.G. Services. No criticism.	
CROWBOROUGH. 2.11.15. 7.0 pm.	Divisional Supply Office inspected by Chief Inspector of Q.M.G. Services. No criticism but various suggestions made by that Officer now being carried out.	
CROWBOROUGH. 3.11.15. 11.0 am.	Supply Depot Inspected by Chief Inspector of Q.M.G. Services. Suggestions made as to Supplies, mode of accounting for reduced ration as set out in 2nd Army. Order dated 7th August 1915. The Suggestions are now being carried out with good results.	
TUNBRIDGE WELLS. 3.11.15. 2.30 pm.	No. 2 Company inspected by the Chief Inspector of Q.M.G. Services.	
TUNBRIDGE WELLS. 3.11.15. 4.0 pm.	Supply Depot inspected by Chief Inspector of C.M.G. Services. No criticism except that the bread was not well enough baked. The Contractor has now been changed and the bread is of excellent quality.	
EAST GRINSTEAD. 5.11.15. 9.30 p.m.	No. 1 Company received 50 Heavy Draught Horses from Amesbury.	
CROWBOROUGH. 6.11.15.	No. 4 Company received 15 Heavy Draught Horses.	
EAST GRINSTEAD. 9.11.15. 8.30 pm.	No. 1 Company received 39 Heavy Draught Horses from Romsey.	
CROWBOROUGH. 15.11.15. 11.30 am.	Lt.General Woolacombe C.B. & Major General Blomfield C.B. D.S.O. inspected No. 3 Company in Column of Route just outside the Camp afterwards visiting the Stables, Officers Mess, Kitchens (Cook House) & Hutments.	
EAST GRINSTEAD. 15.11.15. 1.30 pm.	Inspection of No. 1 Company's Horses & Wagons by G.O.C., 2nd Army. Central Force.	

WAR DIARY
or
INTELLIGENCE SUMMARY

(Erase heading not required.)

Army Form C. 2118

Instructions regarding War Diaries and Intelligence Summaries are contained in F. S. Regs., Part II. and the Staff Manual respectively. Title Pages will be prepared in manuscript.

Place	Date	Hour	Summary of Events and Information	Remarks and references to Appendices
East Grinstead	2/11/15	3.30 p.m.	Inspection of Horses, Wagons by Chief Inspector 2 M.G. Services	
"	5/11/15	9.30 a.m.	Received 50 Heavy Draught Horses from Shrewsbury.	
"	9/11/15	8.30 a.m.	Received 39 Heavy Draught Horses from Romsey.	
"	10/11/15	1.30 p.m.	Inspection of Horses & Wagons by G.O.C. 2nd Army Central Force	
"	23/11/15		Received 4 Mark X Wagons G.S. from Lincoln.	

East Grinstead
30/11/15

S.P. Humphreys Major
H: 1 Coy 66 (East Lancs) Divl A.S.C.

Army Form C. 2118.

WAR DIARY
or
INTELLIGENCE SUMMARY.
(*Erase heading not required.*)

Instructions regarding War Diaries and Intelligence Summaries are contained in F.S. Regs., Part II. and the Staff Manual respectively. Title pages will be prepared in manuscript.

Hour, Date, Place		Summary of Events and Information	Remarks and references to Appendices
CROWBOROUGH.	20.11.15. 11.45 pm.	Officers Mess of the 2/5th Battn. East Lancs. Regiment Burnt down.	
CROWBOROUGH.	20.11.15.	At 12. midnight a fire broke out in the lines of the 2/5th Battalion East Lancs. Regiment and O.C. No. 4 Company proceeded there with a Fire Picquet.	
EAST GRINSTEAD.	23.11.15.	No. 1 Company received 4 Mark X Wagons G.S. from Lincoln.	

signature
Lt-Colonel,
Commdg. 66th (East Lancs.) Div. Train.

Army Form C. 2118.

WAR DIARY
or
INTELLIGENCE SUMMARY.

(*Erase heading not required.*)

Instructions regarding War Diaries and Intelligence Summaries are contained in F.S. Regs., Part II. and the Staff Manual respectively. Title pages will be prepared in manuscript.

Hour, Date, Place		Summary of Events and Information	Remarks and references to Appendices
CROWBOROUGH. 20.11.15.	11.45 pm.	Officers Mess of the 2/5th Battn. East Lancs. Regiment Burnt down.	
CROWBOROUGH. 20.11.15.		At 12. midnight a fire broke out in the lines of the 2/5th Battalion East Lancs. Regiment and O.C. No. 4 Company proceeded there with a Fire Picquet.	
EAST GRINSTEAD. 23.11.15.		No. 1 Company received 4 Mark X Wagons G.S. from Lincoln.	

[signature] Lt-Colonel,
Commdg. 66th (East Lancs.) Div. Train.

(9 29 6) W 4141—453 100,000 5/14 H W V Forms/C. 2118/10

Army Form C. 2118

WAR DIARY
or
INTELLIGENCE SUMMARY
(Erase heading not required.)

Instructions regarding War Diaries and Intelligence Summaries are contained in F. S. Regs., Part II. and the Staff Manual respectively. Title Pages will be prepared in manuscript.

Place	Date	Hour	Summary of Events and Information	Remarks and references to Appendices
East Grinstead	2/11/15	3.30 p.m.	Inspection of Horses & Wagons by Chief Inspector 2 M.G. Service.	
"	5/11/15	9.30 a.m.	Received 50 Heavy Draught Horses from Shrewsbury.	
"	9/11/15	8.30 a.m.	Received 39 Heavy Draught Horses from Romsey.	
"	18/11/15	1.30 p.m.	Inspection of Horses & Wagons by G.O.C. 2nd Army, Central Force	
"	23/11/15		Received 4 Mark I Wagons G.S. from Lincoln.	

East Grinstead
30/11-15"

R. Hughes Major
Wirby 66 (East Lancs) Divl A.S.C.

WAR DIARY
or
INTELLIGENCE SUMMARY

(Erase heading not required.)

Army Form C. 2118

Instructions regarding War Diaries and Intelligence Summaries are contained in F.S. Regs., Part II. and the Staff Manual respectively. Title Pages will be prepared in manuscript.

Place	Date	Hour	Summary of Events and Information	Remarks and references to Appendices
[illegible]			No event of importance to record during the month of December 1915.	ML

H. Hewlett Capt
16 sub Coy
No 1 Coast Defence Searchlights

Army Form C. 2118

WAR DIARY
or
INTELLIGENCE SUMMARY
(Erase heading not required.)

Instructions regarding War Diaries and Intelligence Summaries are contained in F. S. Regs., Part II. and the Staff Manual respectively. Title Pages will be prepared in manuscript.

Place	Date	Hour	Summary of Events and Information	Remarks and references to Appendices
			No event of importance to record during the month of December 1915.	

(Sgd.) J. Stanhope
Lt-Colonel,
Commdg. 66th (East Lancs.) Div. Train.

Army Form C. 2118.

WAR DIARY
or
INTELLIGENCE SUMMARY.
(*Erase heading not required.*)

Hour, Date, Place	Summary of Events and Information	Remarks and references to Appendices
HARTFIELD 20.1.16. 12 noon.	The Train concentrated at HARTFIELD and was inspected by A.D.S.& T. 2nd Army, Central Force. A favourable report was received.	T.B.L.
	T.B. Doyle, Major for Lt-Colonel, Commdg. 66th (East Lancs.) Div. Train.	

Army Form C. 2118.

WAR DIARY
or
INTELLIGENCE SUMMARY.
(Erase heading not required.)

Instructions regarding War Diaries and Intelligence Summaries are contained in F.S. Regs., Part II. and the Staff Manual respectively. Title pages will be prepared in manuscript.

Hour, Date, Place	Summary of Events and Information	Remarks and references to Appendices
12 NOON 16-2-16 CROWBOROUGH.	Train concentrated on MARESFIELD – HARTFIELD road with head at fork roads S. of 37th milestone (Ref 1" Ord. Sur. Map(b 126)	

signature

Lt-Colonel,
Commdg. 66th (East Lancs.) Div. Train.

WAR DIARY
or
INTELLIGENCE SUMMARY.
(Erase heading not required.)

Army Form C. 2118.

Hour, Date, Place	Summary of Events and Information	Remarks and references to Appendices
HARTFIELD 20.1.16. 12 noon.	The train concentrated at HARTFIELD and was inspected by A.D.S.&T. 2nd Army, Central Force. A favourable report was received. T.B. Lyle. Major for Lt-Colonel, Commdg. 66th (East Lancs.) Div. Train.	T.B.L.

Army Form C. 2118.

WAR DIARY

~~INTELLIGENCE SUMMARY~~

(Erase heading not required.)

February 1916.

Place	Date	Hour	Summary of Events and Information	Remarks and references to Appendices
			Nil return.	

Edward Faed
CAPTAIN
COMMANDING No. 542 COY.
66th (EAST LANCS.) DIVL. TRAIN, A.S.C.

Instructions regarding War Diaries and Intelligence Summaries are contained in F. S. Regs., Part II. and the Staff Manual respectively. Title pages will be prepared in manuscript.

Army Form C. 2118.

WAR DIARY
or
INTELLIGENCE SUMMARY.
(Erase heading not required.)

Instructions regarding War Diaries and Intelligence Summaries are contained in F.S. Regs., Part II. and the Staff Manual respectively. Title pages will be prepared in manuscript.

Hour, Date, Place	Summary of Events and Information	Remarks and references to Appendices
12 noon 16-2-16 CROWBOROUGH.	Train concentrated on MARESFIELD — HARTFIELD road with head at fork roads S. of 37td milestone (Ref 1" Ord. Sur. Map No 126)	

T. Mackenzie
Lt-Colonel,
Commdg. 66th (East Lancs.) Div. Train.

MONTHLY STATEMENT RENDERED IN CONNECTION

WITH WAR DIARIES.

541 Coy /nn Nov 15

Unit. No. 1 Company, 66th.(East Lancs.) Divl. A.S.C.

Division. 66th. (East Lancashire) Division.

Mobilization Centre. Manchester.

Temporary War Station. Crowborough.

Stations since occupied subsequent to mobilization. Bury, Huyton, Southport, and Crowborough.

Training. This has been carried out in a very satisfactory manner and the men show a marked improvement. During the month a cold shoeing class was held, and at the completion of same, an examination was held showing very good results.

Discipline. The discipline of the Camp has been good, and considering the large number of horses the men have had to look after, there has been very little grumbling and they have worked well.

Ordnance Service. Equipment is now coming forward much better, and during the month I received 63 sets of harness.

Transport. This has been carried out well and all the work performed satisfactorily, with no complaints. The Supply Section has been carried out in a satisfactory manner.

Crowborough.
2-9-15.

R. Simpson
Major.
66th. (East Lancs.) Division.

Army Form C. 2118.

WAR DIARY

~~INTELLIGENCE SUMMARY~~

February 1916.

(Erase heading not required.)

Instructions regarding War Diaries and Intelligence Summaries are contained in F. S. Regs., Part II. and the Staff Manual respectively. Title pages will be prepared in manuscript.

Place	Date	Hour	Summary of Events and Information	Remarks and references to Appendices
			Nil return.	

Edward Hood
CAPTAIN
COMMANDING No. 542 COY.
66th (EAST LANCS.) DIV'L. TRAIN, A.S.C.

Army Form C. 2118

541 Coy ASC from Nov 1915

WAR DIARY
or
INTELLIGENCE SUMMARY
(Erase heading not required.)

Instructions regarding War Diaries and Intelligence Summaries are contained in F. S. Regs, Part II. and the Staff Manual respectively. Title Pages will be prepared in manuscript.

Place	Date	Hour	Summary of Events and Information	Remarks and references to Appendices
Crowborough.	4/10/15.		Sent a Convoy to Pease Pottage, consisting of 11 Wagons, 4 Riding Horses, and 22 Heavy Draught Horses.	
do.	14/10/15.	10.0 a.m.	Removed from Crowborough to East Grinstead with 3 Officers, 98 N.C.O's and Men. 15 Wagons and 2 Carts, 11 Riding Horses and 33 Heavy draught horses.	
E.Grinstead.	14/10/15.	4.0 p.m.	Arrived with above Convoy.	
do.	15/10/15.		Sent a Convoy to Crowborough consisting of 8 Wagons, 2 Riding Horses, and 16 Heavy Draught Horses.	
do.	17/10/15.		Sent two men to the Cold Shoeing Class at Bermondsey.	

EAST GRINSTEAD.
31st October 1915.

S. Simpson
Major.
O.C. No. 1 Company,
66th (East Lancs) Div. A.S.C.

WAR DIARY
or
INTELLIGENCE SUMMARY

Army Form C. 2118

Place	Date	Hour	Summary of Events and Information	Remarks and references to Appendices
East Grinstead	4-12-15		Took over command of No 1 Co. 66th (East Lancs) Divisional Train A.S.C. from Major C.E. Simpson.	
	9-12-15		Received visit from Major K.D. McKenzie who had taken over command of the Train.	
	14-12-15		Received visit from Major McKenzie who inspected Stables, N.C.Os, rides and gave a lecture to Officers and N.C.Os.	
	14-12-15	6.15am	Received 15 N.R. Horses from Tidworth, in a very bad condition.	
	18-12-15		3 horses (2 Riders, 1 D.) handed over to R.F.A.	
	18-12-15		1 N.D. horse sent to Veterinary Hospital Tunbridge Wells.	
	19-12-15	4.56am	Received 14 N.R. horses, part of consignment of 18, from 16th Bn. Cheshire Regt. the other 14 were sent to 54th Divisional Train.	
	20-12-15		Received visit from C.O., inspected Stables and men and gave a lecture to Officers and N.C.Os	
	27-12-15		Received 10 Wagons & S. mark X from 199th Infantry Brigade.	
	31-12-15		Received 10 Wagons & S. mark X from R.F.A.	
	31-12-15		Sent 1 Wagon & S. Brown to Mobile Veterinary Section.	
			During the month the Company has now practically the entire transport of supplies to Forest Row as well as fetching any requisitions for transport including the move of the 2/4th (Stonikyr) Brigade from Forest Row to Maresfield. Mobilization equipment is coming in steadily.	

G.O. Taylor
Captain
OC No 1 Company,
66th (East Lancashire) Divisional Army Service Corps.

Army Form C. 2118

WAR DIARY
or
INTELLIGENCE SUMMARY

(Erase heading not required.)

541 Coy ASC from Nov 1915

Instructions regarding War Diaries and Intelligence Summaries are contained in F.S. Regs., Part II. and the Staff Manual respectively. Title Pages will be prepared in manuscript.

Place	Date	Hour	Summary of Events and Information	Remarks and references to Appendices
Crowborough.	4/10/15.		Sent a Convoy to Pease Pottage, consisting of 11 Wagons, 4 Riding Horses, and 22 Heavy Draught Horses.	
do.	14/10/15.	10.0 a.m.	Removed from Crowborough to East Grinstead with 3 Officers, 98 N.C.O's and Men. 15 Wagons and 2 Carts, 11 Riding Horses and 33 Heavy draught horses.	
Grinstead.	14/10/15.	4.0 p.m.	Arrived with above Convoy.	
do.	15/10/15.		Sent a Convoy to Crowborough consisting of 8 Wagons, 2 Riding Horses, and 16 Heavy Draught Horses.	
do.	17/10/15.		Sent two men to the Cold Shoeing Class at Bermondsey.	

EAST GRINSTEAD.
31st October 1915.

SSimpson
Major.
O.C. No. 1 Company,
66th (East Lancs) Div. A.S.C.

Army Form C. 2118

WAR DIARY
or
INTELLIGENCE SUMMARY

(Erase heading not required.)

Instructions regarding War Diaries and Intelligence Summaries are contained in F.S. Regs., Part II. and the Staff Manual respectively. Title Pages will be prepared in manuscript.

Place	Date	Hour	Summary of Events and Information	Remarks and references to Appendices
E. Grinstead			Concentration march to HARTFIELD (Ref. 1" Ordnance Survey map Sheet 126) March through SMALLFIELD & HORLEY and back through COPTHORNE	Sy. G.T. 14/3 BT
	9 Jan'y			

G.Q.Taylor
CAPTAIN,
COMMANDING No. 541 COMPANY,
60TH (2ND LONDON) DIVISIONAL TRAIN, A.S.C.

Army Form C. 2118

WAR DIARY
or
INTELLIGENCE SUMMARY
(Erase heading not required.)

Instructions regarding War Diaries and Intelligence Summaries are contained in F.S. Regs., Part II. and the Staff Manual respectively. Title Pages will be prepared in manuscript.

Place	Date	Hour	Summary of Events and Information	Remarks and references to Appendices
Grimstead	4-12-15		Took over command of No. 1 Co. 66th (East Lancs.) Divisional Train A.S.C. from Major E. E. Simpson.	
	9-12-15		Received visit from Major K. D. McKenzie who had taken over command of the Train.	
	14-12-15		Received visit from Major McKenzie who inspected Stables, H.C.O's mess and gave a lecture to Officers and N.C.O's.	
	17-12-15 6.15am		Received 15 N.D. Horses from Tidworth, in a very bad condition.	
	18-12-15		3 horses (2 Riders, 1 L.D.) handed over to R.F.A.	
	18-12-15		1 N.D. Horse sent to Veterinary Hospital Tunbridge Wells.	
	19-12-15 4.56am		Received 4 N.D. horses part of consignment of 18, from 16th Bn. Cheshire Regt. the other 14 were sent to 54th Divisional Train.	
	20-12-15		Received visit from C.O., inspected Stables and men and gave a lecture to Officers and N.C.O's.	
	27-12-15		Received 10 Wagons G.S. mark X from 199th Infantry Brigade.	
	31-12-15		Received 10 Wagons G.S. mark X from R.F.A.	
	31-12-15		Sent 1 Wagon G.S. Barn to Mobile Veterinary Section.	
			During the month the Company has now practically the entire transport of supplies to Forest Row as well as taking my requisitions for transport including the move of the 2/4th (Hornsey) Brigade from Forest Row to Maresfield. Mobilization equipment is coming in steadily.	

G. D. Taylor
CAPTAIN.
O.C. No. 1 COMPANY,
66TH (EAST LANCASHIRE DIVISIONAL) ARMY SERVICE CORPS.

WAR DIARY

~~INTELLIGENCE SUMMARY~~

(Erase heading not required.)

Army Form C. 2118

Place	Date	Hour	Summary of Events and Information	Remarks and references to Appendices
Grinstead	16.2.16		Train concentrated on MARESFIELD – HARTFIELD road with head at fork roads S of 37th milestone (Reference 1" Ord. Sur. Map. Sheet 126)	G.T.

G. G. Taylor
Lt. Franc
S.41 6° A.S.C.

Army Form C. 2118

WAR DIARY
or
INTELLIGENCE SUMMARY
(Erase heading not required.)

Instructions regarding War Diaries and Intelligence Summaries are contained in F. S. Regs., Part II. and the Staff Manual respectively. Title Pages will be prepared in manuscript.

Place	Date	Hour	Summary of Events and Information	Remarks and references to Appendices
Springlots		7 am 1	Concentration march to HARTFIELD (Ref. 1" Ordnance Survey map sheet 126) march through SMALLFIELD, HORLEY and back through COPTHORNE	eg.O.T. eg. O.T.

E.Q.Taylor
CAPTAIN,
COMMANDING No. 541 COMPANY,
60th (2nd LANCS.) DIVISIONAL TRAIN, A.S.C

542 Coy ASC
from Dec 1915

MONTHLY STATEMENT IN CONNECTION

WITH

WAR DIARIES.

UNIT.   66th (East Lancs) Div. A.S.C.

   No. 2 Company.

~~DIVISION~~.   66th (East Lancsashire).

MOBILIZATION CENTRE.   Manchester. Lancs.

TEMPORARY WAR STATION.   Crowborough, Sussex.

STATIONS. since occupied subsequent to concentration

   Turton, Lancs.   Huyton, Lancs.

   Southport, Lancs.   Crowborough, Sussex.

(b)

CONCENTRATION AT WAR STATIONS.

   Two Officers - Twenty five N.C.O s and men, and twelve horses left this Camp on August 8th for Maidstone in connection with the supply of the Lancashire Fusilier Brigade, who are temporarily stationed there.
   The journey was made by road.
   The above returned to Camp by road on the 30th August 1915.

TRAINING.

   We are now in possession of half establishment of horses and almost the entire establishment of Harness, and great progress has been made during the past month, in the general training of the N.C.Os and men.

(e) DISCIPLINE.

   The general discipline remains good.

(c) ORGANISATION FOR DEFENCE.

   On August 9th 1915 in accordance with instructions all Rifles and Ammunition were returned to Ordnance.

(f) ADMINISTRATION.

   We have received thirteen extra horses during the month, and 22 double sets of Ride and Drive Harness, we are now able to turn out half of our total establishment of transport.

Crowborough
4th Sept 1915

Army Form C. 2118

WAR DIARY
or
~~INTELLIGENCE SUMMARY~~

(Erase heading not required.)

Instructions regarding War Diaries and Intelligence Summaries are contained in F. S. Regs., Part II. and the Staff Manual respectively. Title Pages will be prepared in manuscript.

Place	Date	Hour	Summary of Events and Information	Remarks and references to Appendices
Grinstead	16-2-16		Train concentrated on MARESFIELD — HARTFIELD road with head at forks roads S of 37th milestone (Reference 1" Ord. Sur. map Sheet 126)	Ap. 9t

E. G. Taylor
Captain
54½ 6° A.S.C.

542 COY ASC
From Dec 1915

Army Form C. 2118.

WAR DIARY
-of-
INTELLIGENCE SUMMARY.
(Erase heading not required.)

Instructions regarding War Diaries and Intelligence Summaries are contained in F. S. Regs., Part II. and the Staff Manual respectively. Title pages will be prepared in manuscript.

Place	Date	Hour	Summary of Events and Information	Remarks and references to Appendices
Crowborough	Oct 1915 14th	8.45 a.m.	No 1 Company A.S.C. left the Camp and proceeded by March route to East Grinstead.	
	18th 19th 20th	8 a.m.	Convoys left daily for Tunbridge Wells with stores etc. of the 19th Infantry Brigade.	
	21st	7 a.m.	We left Crowborough Camp for new Quarters at Tunbridge Wells by Route March - arrived at new quarters (10 St James Rd Comp office) at 11 oclock proceeded to unload kits, stores, etc. N.C.O. and men billeted in empty houses with Central fusing.	
Tunbridge Wells	29th	7 a.m.	Convoy left for Buxton Camp to bring stores etc to Crowborough the night was spent at Buxton Camp - the night of the 30th at Tonbridge Convoy returned to Tunbridge Wells on Sunday 31st inst at 11 a.m. & the wagons were taken on to Crowborough by No 3 Comp A.S.C.	

Tunbridge Wells. 31-X-15

Gerard Fox
CAPT.
COMMANDING NO. 2 COY.
66th (EAST LANCS) DIV. A.S.C.

Army Form C. 2118.

WAR DIARY
or
INTELLIGENCE SUMMARY.

November 1915.

(Erase heading not required.)

Instructions regarding War Diaries and Intelligence Summaries are contained in F. S. Regs., Part II. and the Staff Manual respectively. Title pages will be prepared in manuscript.

Place	Date	Hour	Summary of Events and Information	Remarks and references to Appendices.
...bridge ...ells.	3rd	2.30 p.m.	The Company was inspected by the Chief Inspector of L. of C. Services.	

[Signature] CAPT.
COMMANDING No. 2 COY.
66th (EAST LANCS.) DIV. A.S.C.

542 COY ASC
From Dec 1915

Army Form C. 2118.

WAR DIARY
INTELLIGENCE SUMMARY.
(Erase heading not required.)

Instructions regarding War Diaries and Intelligence Summaries are contained in F. S. Regs., Part II. and the Staff Manual respectively. Title pages will be prepared in manuscript.

Place	Date	Hour	Summary of Events and Information	Remarks and references to Appendices
...borough	Oct 1915 14th	8.45 a.m.	No 1 Company A.S.C. left the Camp and proceeded by march route to East Grinstead.	
	18th 19th 20th	8 a.m.	Convoys left daily for Tunbridge Wells with Stores etc. of the 197th Infantry Brigade.	
	21st	7 a.m.	We left Crowborough Camp for new Quarters at Tunbridge Wells by Route March - arrived at new quarters (10 St James Rd Comp office) at 11 oclock proceeded to unload kits, Stores etc. N.C.O and men billeted in empty houses with Central feeding.	
...idge Wells	29-	7 a.m.	Convoy left for Buxton Camp to bring Stores etc to Crowborough the night was spent at Buxton Camp - the night of the 30th at Tonbridge Convoy returned to Tunbridge Wells on Sunday 31st inst at 11 a.m. & the wagons were taken on to Crowborough by No 3 Comp A.S.C.	

Tunbridge Wells. 31-X-15

[signature]
Capt.
COMMANDING No. 2 COY.
66th (EAST LANCS.) DIV. A.S.C.

Army Form C. 2118.

WAR DIARY
or
~~INTELLIGENCE SUMMARY.~~
(Erase heading not required.)

December 1915

Instructions regarding War Diaries and Intelligence Summaries are contained in F. S. Regs., Part II. and the Staff Manual respectively. Title pages will be prepared in manuscript.

Place	Date	Hour	Summary of Events and Information	Remarks and references to Appendices
	1915			
Erquinghem Lys	6/12/15	2 p.m.	Alarm sounded and Company paraded. All horses and wagons Reported all correct and ready to move to Brigade at 2.30 p.m. & dismissed	
"	10/12/15	10.30 p.m.	Alarm sounded all men of the Company were turned out on parade. Reported correct 11-10 p.m. & dismissed.	
"	16/12/15	11.5 p.m.	Alarm sounded and Company paraded. All horses and wagons Reported all correct and ready to move to Brigade at 12 p.m. & dismissed 2 a.m.	

Gerard Read
CAPTAIN,
COMMANDING No. 542 COY.
66th (EAST LANCS.) DIVL. TRAIN, A.S.C.

T.134. Wt. W708—776. 500000. 4/15. Sir J. C. & S.

WAR DIARY
~~INTELLIGENCE~~ SUMMARY.

November 1915.

(Erase heading not required.)

Army Form C. 2118.

Instructions regarding War Diaries and Intelligence Summaries are contained in F. S. Regs., Part II. and the Staff Manual respectively. Title pages will be prepared in manuscript.

Place	Date	Hour	Summary of Events and Information	Remarks and references to Appendices
Tonbridge Wells	3rd	2.30 p.m.	The Company was inspected by the Chief Inspector of L. of C. Mr. General Services.	

Bernard Ward CAPT.,
COMMANDING NO. 2 COY.
66th (EAST LANCS.) DIV. A.S.C.

Army Form C. 2118.

WAR DIARY
INTELLIGENCE SUMMARY.
(Erase heading not required.)

Place	Date	Hour	Summary of Events and Information	Remarks and references to Appendices
Tunbridge Wells	31.1.16		Nil	

R.M.Simpson Lt.
Actg. O.C.
No. 542 Coy. A.P.C.

Instructions regarding War Diaries and Intelligence Summaries are contained in F. S. Regs., Part II. and the Staff Manual respectively. Title pages will be prepared in manuscript.

WAR DIARY or INTELLIGENCE SUMMARY.

Army Form C. 2118.

December 1915

Place	Date	Hour	Summary of Events and Information	Remarks and references to Appendices
	1915			
Briage Wells	6/12/15	2 p.m.	Alarm sounded and Company paraded. - All horses and wagons Reported all correct and ready to move to Brigadier at 2.30 p.m. & dismissed	
"	10/12/15	10.30 p.m.	Alarm sounded all men of the Company were turned out on parade. - Reported correct 11.10 p.m. & dismissed.	
"	16/12/15	11.5 p.m.	Alarm sounded and Company paraded. - All horses and wagons Reported all correct and ready to move to Brigadier at 12 p.m. & dismissed 2. a.m.	

Greenfield
CAPTAIN,
COMMANDING No. 542 COY.
66th (EAST LANCS.) DIVL TRAIN, A.S.C.

WAR DIARY

INTELLIGENCE SUMMARY

February 1916

Army Form C. 2118.

(Erase heading not required.)

Instructions regarding War Diaries and Intelligence Summaries are contained in F. S. Regs., Part II. and the Staff Manual respectively. Title pages will be prepared in manuscript.

Place	Date	Hour	Summary of Events and Information	Remarks and references to Appendices
			Nil return.	

[Signed] Captain,
COMMANDING No. 542 COY.
86th (EAST LANCS.) DIVL. TRAIN, A.S.C.

Army Form C. 2118.

WAR DIARY
INTELLIGENCE SUMMARY
(Erase heading not required.)

Place	Date	Hour	Summary of Events and Information	Remarks and references to Appendices
Tunbridge Wells	31.1.16		Nil	

Instructions regarding War Diaries and Intelligence Summaries are contained in F. S. Regs., Part II. and the Staff Manual respectively. Title pages will be prepared in manuscript.

R M Simpson Lt.
Actg. O.C.
No. 542 Coy. A.P.C.

543 COY ASC
Transport DEC 1915

War Diary Statement

Unit	No 3 Coy 66th (East Lancs) Divisional A.S.C
Brigade	198th Infantry Brigade (attached to)
Division	66th (East Lancs) Division
Mobilization Centre	Hulme Barracks, Manchester
Tempy War Station	Pease Pottage Camp
Stations occupied subsequent to Concentration	Bury, Huyton, Southport, Haywards Heath, Pease Pottage

(a) Mobilization —

(b) Concentration at War Station — No war station yet allotted

(c) Organisation for defence — None no rifles in possession of unit

(d) Training — Being proceeded with as quickly as possible

(e) Discipline — Very good

(f) Administration
   (1) Medical Services — good
   (2) Veterinary Services — civilian good
   (3) Supply Services — very good
   (4) Transport Services — Improving as harness has now been received
   (5) Ordnance Services — Unsatisfactory
   (6) Billeting & Hutting — This unit is under Canvas, satisfactory
   (7) Channels of correspondence in routine matters — Divisional Headquarters, Lea House, Crowborough
   (8) Range Construction — Does not apply to this unit
   (9) Supply of Remounts — Supply as regards quantity is satisfactory but not as regards quality.

(g) Reorganisation of T.F. into home and Imperial Service — This unit consists of Imperial Service Men only

(h) Preparation of unit for Imperial Service — This unit is supplying the 198th Infantry Brigade 2/3rd Field Ambulance R.A.M.C. 1 Section 2/1st Royal Engineers. also all necessary 2nd line transport for the 198th Infantry Brigade is being done

H. Henshall CAPTAIN,
OFFICER COMMANDING No 3 Coy

WAR DIARY

INTELLIGENCE SUMMARY

(Erase heading not required.)

February 1916

Army Form C. 2118.

Instructions regarding War Diaries and Intelligence Summaries are contained in F.S. Regs., Part II. and the Staff Manual respectively. Title pages will be prepared in manuscript.

Place	Date	Hour	Summary of Events and Information	Remarks and references to Appendices
			Nil return.	

Edward Read
CAPTAIN,
COMMANDING No. 542 COY.
66th (EAST LANCS.) DIVL. TRAIN, A.S.C.

543 Coy ASC
from Sep 15

No. 3 COY. 66th (EAST LANCS.)
DIVISIONAL TRAIN
Date 2.10.15

Army Form C. 2118.

WAR DIARY
or
INTELLIGENCE SUMMARY.
(Erase heading not required.)

Instructions regarding War Diaries and Intelligence Summaries are contained in F. S. Regs., Part II. and the Staff Manual respectively. Title pages will be prepared in manuscript.

Place	Date	Hour	Summary of Events and Information	Remarks and references to Appendices
Pea Pottage Camp	21/9/15	3.30pm	Unit left Pea Pottage Camp for Maidstone via East Grinstead & Tonbridge	
E. Grinstead	21/9/15	7.15pm	Unit arrived East Grinstead	
E. Grinstead	22/9/15	9.0 a.z.	Unit left East Grinstead for Tonbridge	
Tonbridge	22/9/15	6.0 p.z.	Unit arrived at Tonbridge	
Tonbridge	23/9/15	9.0 a.z.	Unit left Tonbridge	
Maidstone	23/9/15	4.0 p.z.	Unit arrived at Maidstone	

H. Newshall
CAPTAIN,
OFFICER COMMANDING No 3 Coy
A.S.C.

WAR DIARY or INTELLIGENCE SUMMARY.

Army Form C. 2118.

(Erase heading not required.)

Hour, Date, Place	Summary of Events and Information	Remarks and References to Appendices
11 a.m. 20/10/15 Maidstone	No 3 Company Horse Transport left Maidstone for Tunbridge Wells arriving 5.30 p.m.	
5.30 a.m. 21/10/15 Tunbridge Wells	No 3 Company Horse Transport left Tunbridge Wells for Crowborough arriving 1.0 p.m.	
5.30 p.m. 24/10/15 Maidstone	No 3 Company Supply Section left Maidstone for Crowborough arriving 7.30 p.m.	

F. H. Newhall, Captain,
O/C No. 3 Company,
66. East Lancs A.S.C.

Army Form C. 2118

WAR DIARY
or
INTELLIGENCE SUMMARY
(Erase heading not required.)

Instructions regarding War Diaries and Intelligence Summaries are contained in F.S. Regs., Part II. and the Staff Manual respectively. Title Pages will be prepared in manuscript.

Place	Date	Hour	Summary of Events and Information	Remarks and references to Appendices
Edinburgh	7/10/15	10.45 a.m.	Major General F.H.B. Landon C.B. inspected No 3 Coy to ascertain if work on the Mansfield load route from camp. Mansure (pittings) + condition of horses was entered. Efforts are now being made to remedy defects complained of.	M.H.
Edinburgh	3/11/15	11.45 a.m.	Major General M.B. Landon C.B. inspected the lines of No 3 Coy afterwards visiting stables, took horses that the condition of the stables was achieved. materials are being provided by the R.O.H.S. to improve the stables.	M.H.
Edinburgh	15/11/15	11.30 a.m.	Lt General Hookewade C.B + Major General Blomfield C.B.D.C inspected No 3 Coy in charge of horses first entered the camp afterwards visiting the stables, officer mess, kitchens (cook house) shelves	M.H.
Edinburgh	30/11/15	11.45 a.m.	Officers mess of the 75th Bttn East Lanen Regt. Burnt down	M.H.

W. Kendall Capt.
O.C. No 3 Coy
W.E. Lanc. Divid Train

1875 Wt. W593/826 1,000,000 4/15 J.B.C. & A. A.D.S.S./Forms/C. 2118.

Army Form C. 2118.

WAR DIARY
or
INTELLIGENCE SUMMARY.
(Erase heading not required.)

Instructions regarding War Diaries and Intelligence Summaries are contained in F. S. Regs., Part II. and the Staff Manual respectively. Title pages will be prepared in manuscript.

Hour, Date, Place	Summary of Events and Information	Remarks and References to Appendices
1 a.m. 20/10/15 Maidstone	No 3 Company Horse transport left Maidstone for Tunbridge Wells arriving 8.30 p.m.	
8.30 a.m. 21/10/15 Tunbridge Wells	No. 3 Company Horse transport left Tunbridge Wells for Crowborough arriving 1.0 p.m.	
30 p.m. 24/10/15 Maidstone	No. 3 Company Supply Section left Maidstone for Crowborough arriving 7.30 p.m.	

H. Newall
CAPTAIN,
O/C No. 3 Company,
1/6 East Lancs A.S.C.

WAR DIARY
or
INTELLIGENCE SUMMARY.

(Erase heading not required.)

Army Form C. 2118.

Place	Date	Hour	Summary of Events and Information	Remarks and references to Appendices
Aldershot	20/1/16	12.30 Noon	543 Coy. inspected by Col. Lynn. A.D. of S+T. and Col. Gordon Steward at Hartford. A satisfactory report was received on the Company.	Nil.

M.J. Clifford, CAPTAIN.
O/C No. 543RD COMPANY, A.S.C. M.T.
for. 66TH (EAST LANCS.) DIVISION

Army Form C. 2118

Instructions regarding War Diaries and Intelligence Summaries are contained in F.S. Regs., Part II. and the Staff Manual respectively. Title Pages will be prepared in manuscript.

WAR DIARY
or
INTELLIGENCE SUMMARY
(Erase heading not required.)

Place	Date	Hour	Summary of Events and Information	Remarks and references to Appendices
Canterbury	7/11/15	10.45 am	Major General H.M.B. Lawson C.B. inspected No 3 Coy in column of route on the Mansfield road 1 mile from camp. Harness (fitting of) & condition of horses were criticised. Efforts are now being made to remedy defects. Complaints of NW.	NW
Canterbury	30/11/15	11.0 am	Major General J.M.B. Lawson C.B. inspected the lines of No 3 Coy afterwards visiting stables, cook houses etc. The condition of the stables was criticised, materials are being provided by the D.O.K.S. to improve the stables.	NW
Canterbury	15/1/16	11.30 am	Lt General Woolcombe C.B. & Major General Blomfield C.B.&O. inspected No 3 Coy in column of route just outside the camp, afterwards visiting the stables, officers mess, Kitchens (cook house) latrines.	NW
Canterbury	30/1/16	11.45 pm	Officers mess of the 45th Bttn East Lancs Regt Burnt down	NW

H. Nendall Capt
O.C. No 3 Coy
16 E Lanc Divl Train

Place	Date	Hour	Summary of Events and Information	Remarks and references to Appendices
borough	26/6/16	5 pm	Handed over company to Capt Ball.	1 A.H.
...boro	26/6/16	5 pm	Taken over Command of 343rd Coy from Capt Marshall & attaches necessary certificate - vide Appendix 1 & also during orders.	A/-
...boro	29/6/16	9-10 am	Phone message received from Topcliffe Headquarters that "Period of Vigilance 2" commenced at 9-0 am.	A/-

Alfred Ball
Captain
O/C No. 343rd Coy
66th (East Lancs) Division

544 Coy ASC
from DEC 1915

War Diary for September 1915.

__Sept. 1st - Sept. 18th 1915.__ No 4 Coy. was during this period at Maidstone, doing duty with 199th Infantry Brigade, stationed at Burham.

__Sunday. Sept. 19th 1915.__: Obeying orders this company proceeded by March Route from Maidstone to Crowborough, completing the journey in one day. Following instructions I left 1 Driver (L/Cpl) & spare man with 2 H.D. Horses & one waggon behind in Maidstone for the purpose of doing the transport for the rear-party of 199th Infantry Brigade. These details returned from Maidstone by March Route on 23rd Sept. 1915.

__Sept. 20th - Sept. 30th 1915.__: This Company was on duty at Crowborough together with Nos. 1 & 2 Coys. A.S.C doing general transport work.

Percy W. At............ Capt.
o/c No. 4 Company
66 (EAST LANCS.) DIV. A.S.C.

The Hutments
Crowborough
4/10/15.

//
WAR DIARY
INTELLIGENCE SUMMARY

(Erase heading not required.)

Army Form C. 2118

Place	Date	Hour	Summary of Events and Information	Remarks and references to Appendices
borough	26/2/16	5 pm	Handed over company to Capt Ball.	
"	26/2/16	6 pm	Taken over command of No 543 Cy from Capt Kendall, necessary certificates vide Appendix 4 also stores &c.	
"	29/2/16	9.10 am	Phone message received from Brigade Headquarters that "Period of Vigilance" commenced at 9.0 am.	

Alex M Ball
CAPTAIN.
O/C No. 543 Co. A.S.C.
66th (EAST LANCS) DIVISION

Statement

Unit: No 4 Coy. 66th (E. Lancs) Div. A.S.C.
Brigade: 199th Brigade
Divison: 66th (East Lancs.)

Mobilisation Centre: Manchester.

Temporary War Station: Maidstone

Stations since occupied subsequent to concentration:—
Littleborough, Huyton, Southport, Crowborough, Maidstone

(a) 20 under strength
(c) In possession of no rifles & ammunition.
(d) Men have been through no course of musketry, otherwise training good.
(e) Good.
(f) (1) good.
    (2) No Army Veterinary surgeon here.
    (3) good.
    (4) good.
    (5) Indents being carried out fairly quickly, but very short of grooming kits.
    (6) Good.
    (7) Good.
    (8) —
    (9) Still short of establishment.
(G) This has been carried out.
(H) Preparation is being carried through quickly.

Percy W. St. Lunt
Capt.
o/c No. 4 Company
66th (East Lancs.) Div. A.S.C.

Army Form C. 2118

WAR DIARY for October 1915.

~~INTELLIGENCE SUMMARY~~

514 Coy ASC
from DEC 1915

(Erase heading not required.)

Instructions regarding War Diaries and Intelligence Summaries are contained in F.S. Regs., Part II. and the Staff Manual respectively. Title Pages will be prepared in manuscript.

Place	Date	Hour	Summary of Events and Information	Remarks and references to Appendices
Scarborough	6/10/15.		Convoy to Pease Pottage, returning 9/10/15.	
- do -	11/10/15.		- do - , returning 13/10/15.	
- do -	18/10/15.		Convoy to Tunbridge Wells, returning same day.	
- do -	19/10/15.		- do - - do -	
- do -	20/10/15.		- do - - do -	
- do -	23/10/15.		Convoy to Burham, Nr Maidstone, returning 26/10/15.	
- do -	28/10/15.		- do - - do - 31/10/15.	
Scarborough October			Two Junior Corporals have attended an advanced course in cold-shoeing at Bermondsey.	
- do -	- do -		One Lance/Corporal is at present attending a course of Musketry at Bisley.	

Percy B. Ost Capt.
O/c No. 4 Company
66 (EAST LANCS) DIV A.S.C.

Army Form C. 2118

WAR DIARY for November 1915.

~~INTELLIGENCE SUMMARY~~

(Erase heading not required.)

Instructions regarding War Diaries and Intelligence Summaries are contained in F. S. Regs., Part II. and the Staff Manual respectively. Title Pages will be prepared in manuscript.

Place	Date	Hour	Summary of Events and Information	Remarks and references to Appendices
Peterborough	6/11		Received a further draft of 15 Heavy Draught Horses.	P.W.O
do -	20/11		At 12 Midnight a fire broke out in the lines of the 25th Battalion East Lancs. Regt. I proceeded there with the Fire Piquet.	P.W.O

Percy C. St ___ Capt.
c/o No. 4 Company
66 (EAST LANCS) DIV/A.S.C.

WAR DIARY
or
INTELLIGENCE SUMMARY

Army Form C. 2118

Instructions regarding War Diaries and Intelligence Summaries are contained in F.S. Regs., Part II. and the Staff Manual respectively. Title Pages will be prepared in manuscript.

(Erase heading not required.)

Place	Date	Hour	Summary of Events and Information	Remarks and references to Appendices
OWBOROUGH	29.2.16	11.15am	Order for 61st "Period of Vigilance" received from O.C. 199' Infantry Brigade	A.C. Wilson Lieut.
"	1-3-16	8.34am	Order "Prepare to move" received from O.C. 199' Infantry Brigade	A.C. Wilson Lieut.
"	1-3-16	11.40am	Train transport moved off and followed in rear of Brigade	A.C. Wilson Lieut.
"	1-3-16	4.55pm	Train transport returned to Camp	A.C. Wilson Lieut.

Percy A. St. Capt.
c/o No. 544 Company A.S.C.
66th (EAST LANCS.) DIVL. TRAIN

Army Form C. 2118

WAR DIARY for November 1915.

~~INTELLIGENCE SUMMARY~~

(Erase heading not required.)

Instructions regarding War Diaries and Intelligence Summaries are contained in F. S. Regs., Part II. and the Staff Manual respectively. Title Pages will be prepared in manuscript.

Place	Date	Hour	Summary of Events and Information	Remarks and references to Appendices
ostorough	6/15		Received a further draft of 15 Heavy Draught Horses.	P.W.O
	20/15		At 12 Midnight a few broke out in the lines of the 75th Battalion East Lancs. Regt. I proceeded there with the Vice Regnet.	P.W.O

Percy C. St. Capt.
c/o No. 4 Company
66 (East Lancs) Div. A.S.C.

Army Form C. 2118

WAR DIARY No 544 Coy A.S.C.
66th (E. Lancs) Division

or INTELLIGENCE SUMMARY

(Erase heading not required.)

December 1915.

Instructions regarding War Diaries and Intelligence Summaries are contained in F.S. Regs., Part II. and the Staff Manual respectively. Title Pages will be prepared in manuscript.

Place	Date	Hour	Summary of Events and Information	Remarks and references to Appendices
Crowton Rae.	1915.		Nil.	

Percy B. St-
c/o No. 544 Company A.S.C.
66th (EAST LANCS.) DIV.

Army Form C. 2118

WAR DIARY
or
INTELLIGENCE SUMMARY
(Erase heading not required.)

Instructions regarding War Diaries and Intelligence Summaries are contained in F. S. Regs., Part II. and the Staff Manual respectively. Title Pages will be prepared in manuscript.

Place	Date	Hour	Summary of Events and Information	Remarks and references to Appendices
OWBOROUGH	2.9.16	11.15am	Order for 65th "Period of Vigilance" received from O.C. 199th Infantry Brigade	A.C. Wilson Lieut-
—"—	1-3-16	8.34am	Order "Prepare to Move" received from O.C. 199th Infantry Brigade	A.C. Wilson Lieut-
—"—	1-3-16	11.40am	Train transport moved off and followed in rear of Brigade	A.C. Wilson Lieut-
—"—	1-3-16	4.55 pm	Train transport returned to Camp	A.C. Wilson Lieut-

Percy S. _____ Capt.
c/o No. 544 Company A.S.C.
66th (EAST LANCS.) DIVL. TRAIN

WAR DIARY for January 1916.

Army Form C. 2118

Instructions regarding War Diaries and Intelligence Summaries are contained in F. S. Regs., Part II. and the Staff Manual respectively. Title Pages will be prepared in manuscript.

(Erase heading not required.)

Place	Date	Hour	Summary of Events and Information	Remarks and references to Appendices
...tfield	20/1/16.	2pm.	No 544 Coy. A.S.C. Transport was inspected by Q.M.S.T. 2nd Army. A satisfactory report was given on the company.	DWO

Percy B. St— Capt.
O/c No. 544 Company A.S.C.
66th (EAST LANCS.) DIVL. TRAIN

WAR DIARY No 544 Coy A.D.

December 1915

66th (2 Lines) Division

Army Form C. 2118

INTELLIGENCE SUMMARY

(Erase heading not required.)

Place	Date	Hour	Summary of Events and Information	Remarks and references to Appendices
Crowton	Dec. 1915.		Nil.	

Percy B. St--- Capt.
c/o No. 544 Company A.D.
66th (EAST LANCS.) DIV. H.Q.

66 DIVISION

SENIOR SUPPLY OFFICER

1915 SEP — 1915 DEC

MONTHLY STATEMENT RENDERED IN CONNECTION WITH
WAR DIARIES FOR AUGUST, 1915.
======

UNIT.- 66th (East Lancs.) Divisional Train.

DIVISION.- 66th (East Lancs.) Division.

MOBILIZATION CENTRES.- Manchester & Cloughfold.

TEMPORARY WAR STATIONS.- Crowborough, Peas Pottage
& Maidstone.

STATIONS SINCE OCCUPIED
SUBSEQUENT TO CONCENTRATION.- Bury, Turton, Littleborough,
Huyton, Southport, Crowborough,
Haywards Heath, Peas Pottage & Maidstone.

(a) MOBILIZATION.- Nil.

(b) CONCENTRATION AT WAR STATION.- Nil.

(c) ORGANIZATION FOR DEFENCE.- Not a defensive unit.
No rifles on charge.

(d) TRAINING.- This is progressing satisfactorily as far
as permitted by the limited supply of
technical equipment. Horses have arrived
in large numbers and the whole of the
transport details are kept fully employed
and trained.
All Supply Services for the Division are
being carried out by the supply details and
these are getting their training in their
duties.

(e) DISCIPLINE.- Good.

(f) ADMINISTRATION.-

(1) MEDICAL Services.- Good. A Medical Officer
attached.
(2) VETERINARY SERVICES.- No Veterinary Officer
attached but duties performed by V.O.
attached to the Division.

(3) SUPPLY SERVICES.- Efficiently carried out and no
delays arise.

(4) TRANSPORT SERVICES.- Still very inadequate but
improving. Horses, wagons and harness have
been received. Twenty four Bain wagons have
been handed over to the 199th Infantry Bde.
Mechanical Transport services are being
carried out by a detachment of No. 373 Coy.
A.S.C. stationed at UCKFIELD.

(5) ORDNANCE SERVICES,- 100 sets of R.A. pattern
harness have been received during the month.
It is still very difficult to obtain necessary equipment.

(6) BILLETING & HUTTING.- Satisfactory. All men not
in huts are now billeted with Central feeding
arrangements.

(7) CHANNELS OF COMMUNICATION.- Through Divisional
Headquarters.

(8) RANGE CONSTRUCTION.- Nil.

(9) SUPPLY OF REMOUNTS.- Satisfactory as to numbers but of very poor quality.

(10) REORGANIZATION OF T.F. INTO HOME AND IMPERIAL SERVICE.- The separation has been effected.

(11) PREPARATION OF UNITS FOR IMPERIAL SERVICE.- Satisfactory.

                                               Lieut.-Col.,
                           Cmdg 66th (East Lancs) Div. A.S.C.

Lea,
  CROWBOROUGH.
    6. 9. 1915.

Army Form C. 2118.

WAR DIARY
or
INTELLIGENCE SUMMARY.
(Erase heading not required.)

Instructions regarding War Diaries and Intelligence Summaries are contained in F.S. Regs., Part II. and the Staff Manual respectively. Title pages will be prepared in manuscript.

Hour, Date, Place	Summary of Events and Information	Remarks and references to Appendices

SEP 1915

8.0 am to 6.0Pm 19.9.1915. Maidstone.	The 199th Brigade Company, 66th (East Lancs) Divisional A.S.C. less a small Supply Detachment, proceeded by march route to MAIDSTONE to CROWBOROUGH.	
3.0pm 19.9.15. TONBRIDGE.	Issues of Supplies made to units of 199th Infantry Brigade having been sent out by convoy from CROWBOROUGH.	
8.30am 21.9.1915 to 9.0pm 25.9.1915. CROWBOROUGH.	A Convoy of 1 Officer, 24 Other ranks, 32 animals and 13 wagons G.S. proceeded to PEAS POTTAGE, loaded up with baggage of the 198th Infantry Brigade, and conveyed this via CRAWLEY, EAST GRINSTEAD, SOUTHBOROUGH, TONBRIDGE and AYLESFORD to BURHAM CAMP. The Baggage was off-loaded and the convoy returned via MAIDSTONE to CROWBOROUGH. Distance traversed 98 miles.	
3.30pm 21.9.1915 to 4.0pm 23.9.1915. PEAS POTTAGE.	The 198th Brigade Company, 66th (EAST LANCS) Divisional A.S.C.(less a small Supply Detachment) proceeded by march route via EAST GRINSTEAD and TONBRIDGE to MAIDSTONE.	
4.0pm 21.9.15 EAST GRINSTEAD.	Part Supply Section 198th Infantry Brigade proceeded from PEAS POTTAGE, made issues of supplies for main body arriving 22nd inst.	
4.0pm 22.9.15 TONBRIDGE.	Part Supply Section 198th Infantry Brigade Company proceeded from EAST GRINSTEAD, made issues for main body arriving 23rd inst.	
4.0pm 23.9.15 MAIDSTONE.	Issues to 198th Infantry Brigade made from Agricultural Hall taken over from Supply Section 199th Infantry Brigade. Supplies taken to BURHAM CAMP.	
24.9.1915 WORTHING.	Supply Depot closed. 1/6th (Cyclist) Batt. Royal Sussex Regt. drawing supplies from SHOREHAM. Capt.R.R.Smethurst proceeded to GODSTONE for duty and details ordered to report to O.C. 45th Provisional Battalion. Margate.	
10.0am 27.9.15. CROWBOROUGH.	Details of 2/1st South Eastern Mounted Brigade supplied with rations from Crowborough Depot.	
2.0. pm 28.9.15. MARESFIELD PARK.	2/1st (Q.O.) Dorset Yeomanry attached to Division for rations.	

Lt-Colonel,
Commdg. 66th (East Lancs.) Div. Train.

Army Form C. 2118

WAR DIARY
or
INTELLIGENCE SUMMARY

(Erase heading not required.)

Instructions regarding War Diaries and Intelligence Summaries are contained in F.S. Regs., Part II. and the Staff Manual respectively. Title Pages will be prepared in manuscript.

Place	Date	Hour	Summary of Events and Information	Remarks and references to Appendices
Marlborough	22/9/15	8.30 a.m.	Proceeded to Rose Cottage in charge of 24 men, 32 animals & 13 wagons, & loaded up the baggage of the 158 Infantry Brigade.	
Rose Cottage	22/9/15	8.30 a.m.	Proceeded via Chawley to East Grinstead, & bivouacked for the night.	
East Grinstead	23/9/15	8.30 a.m.	Proceeded via Southborough to Tonbridge & billeted for the night.	
Tonbridge	24/9/15	8.15	Proceeded via Aylesford to Burham, & delivered the baggage to the 158th Infantry Brigade, then on to Maidstone where we were billeted for the night.	
Maidstone	25/9/15	10.0 a.m.	Left Maidstone, & arrived Southborough 5.0 p.m. Total distance 9.8 miles.	
Southborough	2/10/15			

H. Houghton Major
66th (East Lancs) Field A.S.C.

Army Form C. 2118.

WAR DIARY
INTELLIGENCE SUMMARY.
(Erase heading not required.)

Instructions regarding War Diaries and Intelligence Summaries are contained in F.S. Regs., Part II. and the Staff Manual respectively. Title pages will be prepared in manuscript.

Hour, Date, Place	Summary of Events and Information	Remarks and references to Appendices
	SEP 1915	
8.-0 am to 6.0Pm 19.9.1915. Maidstone.	The 199th Brigade Company, 66th (East Lancs) Divisional A.S.C. less a small Supply Detachment, proceeded by march route to MAIDSTONE to CROWBOROUGH.	
5.0pm 19.9.15. TONBRIDGE.	Issues of Supplies made to units of 199th Infantry Brigade having been sent out by convoy from CROWBOROUGH.	
8.30am 21.9.1915 to 9.0pm 25.9.1915. CROWBOROUGH.	A Convoy of 1 Officer, 24 Other ranks, 32 animals and 12 wagons G.S. proceeded to PEAS POTTAGE, loaded up with baggage of the 198th Infantry Brigade, and conveyed this via CRAWLEY, EAST GRINSTEAD, SOUTHBOROUGH, TONBRIDGE and AYLESFORD to BURHAM CAMP. The Baggage was off-loaded and the convoy returned via MAIDSTONE to CROWBOROUGH. Distance traversed 98 miles.	
3.30pm 21.9.1915 to 4.0pm 23.9.1915. PEAS POTTAGE.	The 198th Brigade Company, 66th (EAST LANCS) Divisional A.S.C.(less a small Supply Detachment) proceeded by march route via EAST GRINSTEAD and TONBRIDGE to MAIDSTONE.	
4.0pm 21.9.15 EAST GRINSTEAD.	Part Supply Section 198th Infantry Brigade proceeded from PEASE POTTAGE, made issues of supplies for main body arriving 22nd inst.	
4.0pm 22.9.15 TONBRIDGE.	Part supply Section 198th Infantry Brigade Company proceeded from EAST GRINSTEAD, made issues for main body arriving 23rd inst.	
4.0pm 23.9.15 MAIDSTONE.	Issues to 198th Infantry Brigade made from Agricultural Hall taken over from Supply Section 199th Infantry Brigade. Supplies taken to BURHAM CAMP.	
24.9.1915 WORTHING.	Supply Depot closed. 1/6th (Cyclist) Batt. Royal Sussex Regt. drawing supplies from SHOREHAM. Capt. R.R. Smethurst proceeded to GODSTONE for duty and details ordered to report to O.C. 45th Provisional Battalion. Margate.	
10.0am 27.9.15 CROWBOROUGH.	Details of 2/1st South Eastern Mounted Brigade supplied with rations from Crowborough Depot.	
2.0. pm 28.9.15. MARKSFIELD PARK.	2/1st (Q.O.) Dorset Yeomanry attached to Division for rations.	

Lt-Colonel,
Commdg. 66th (East Lancs.) Div. Train.

Forms/C. 2118/10

Army Form C. 2118.

WAR DIARY
or
INTELLIGENCE SUMMARY.
(Erase heading not required.)

66 DIV Divnl Supply Officer

Instructions regarding War Diaries and Intelligence Summaries are contained in F. S. Regs., Part II. and the Staff Manual respectively. Title pages will be prepared in manuscript.

Hour, Date, Place	Summary of Events and Information	Remarks and References to Appendices
9.0 a.m. 9.15 MAIDSTONE	Supply Section, 198th Brigade Company returned to CROWBOROUGH. Lieut Clarke A. and 2 N.C.Os remained in MAIDSTONE.	
0 p.m. - 19.9.15. TONBRIDGE	Issues of Supplies made to Units of 199th Infantry Brigade being sent out by convoy from Crowborough.	
0 p.m. 21.9.15. EAST GRINSTEAD	Part Supply Section 198th Infantry Brigade proceeded from PEASE POTTAGE made issues of supplies for main body arriving 22nd inst.	
4 p.m. - 22.9.15. TONBRIDGE	Part Supply Section - 198th Infantry Brigade Company proceeded from EAST GRINSTEAD made issues for main body arriving 23rd inst.	
7 p.m. - 23.9.15. MAIDSTONE.	Issues to 198th Infantry Brigade made from Agricultural Hall taken over from Supply Section 199th Infantry Brigade. Supplies taken to BURHAM CAMP.	
- 9 -15. WORTHING.	Supply Depot closed - 1/6th (Cyclist) Batt. Royal Sussex Regt. drawing supplies from SHOREHAM. Capt R.R. Sturthurst proceeded to GODSTONE for duty and details to report to O.C. 45th Provisional Batt. MARGATE.	

WAR DIARY
or
INTELLIGENCE SUMMARY

(Erase heading not required.)

Army Form C. 2118

Instructions regarding War Diaries and Intelligence Summaries are contained in F.S. Regs., Part II. and the Staff Manual respectively. Title Pages will be prepared in manuscript.

Place	Date	Hour	Summary of Events and Information	Remarks and references to Appendices
Marlborough	21/9/15	8.30 a.m.	Proceeded to Rae Cottage in charge of 24 men, 32 animals & 13 Wagons, & loaded up the baggage of the 198th Infantry Brigade.	
Rae Cottage	22/9/15	8.30 a.m.	Proceeded via Chawley to East-Grinstead, & bivouacked for the night.	
East Grinstead	23/9/15	8.30 a.m.	Proceeded via Southborough to Tonbridge & billeted for the night.	
Tonbridge	24/9/15	8.15 a.m.	Proceeded via Aylesford to Burham, & delivered the baggage to the 198th Infantry Brigade, & then on to Maidstone, where we were billeted for the night.	
Maidstone	25/9/15	10.0 a.m.	Left Maidstone, & arrived Gravesend 5.0 p.m. Total distance 58 miles.	
Gravesend	2/10/15			

H. Hodgson Major
66th (East Lancs) Bgd. R.F.A.

1875 Wt. W593/826 1,000,000 4/15 J.B.C. & A. A.D.S.S./Forms/C. 2118.

Army Form C. 2118.

WAR DIARY
or
INTELLIGENCE SUMMARY.
(Erase heading not required.)

Instructions regarding War Diaries and Intelligence Summaries are contained in F. S. Regs., Part II. and the Staff Manual respectively. Title pages will be prepared in manuscript.

Hour, Date, Place	Summary of Events and Information	Remarks and References to Appendices
0 a.m. 27.9.15. CROWBOROUGH.	Details of 2/1 South Eastern Mounted Brigade supplied with rations from Crowborough Depôt.	
0 p.m. 28.9.15. MARESFIELD PARK	2/1 (Q.O.) Dorset Yeomanry attached to Division for Rations.	

T. R. Doyle. Major,
Senior Supply Officer,
66th (East Lancs.) Division.

Army Form C. 2118.

WAR DIARY
or
INTELLIGENCE SUMMARY.
(Erase heading not required.)

66 Div
Divnl Supply Officer

Instructions regarding War Diaries and Intelligence Summaries are contained in F. S. Regs, Part II. and the Staff Manual respectively. Title pages will be prepared in manuscript.

Hour, Date, Place	Summary of Events and Information	Remarks and References to Appendices
9.15 MAIDSTONE	Supply Section, 198th Brigade Company returned to CROWBOROUGH. Lieut Clarke A. and 2 N.C.Os remained in MAIDSTONE.	
p.m. 19.9.15. TONBRIDGE	Issues of Supplies made to Units of 199th Infantry Brigade being sent out by convoy from Crowborough.	
p.m. 21.9.15. EAST GRINSTEAD	Part Supply Section 198th Infantry Brigade proceeded from PEASE POTTAGE made issues of supplies for main body arriving 22nd inst.	
p.m. 22.9.15. TONBRIDGE	Part Supply Section 198th Infantry Brigade Company proceeded from EAST GRINSTEAD made issues for main body arriving 23rd inst.	
p.m. 23.9.15. MAIDSTONE.	Issues to 198th Infantry Brigade made from Agricultural Hall taken over from Supply Section 199th Infantry Brigade. Supplies taken to BURHAM CAMP.	
- 9.15. WORTHING.	Supply Depot closed - 1/6th (Cyclist) Batt. Royal Sussex Regt. drawing Supplies from SHOREHAM. Capt R.R. Swathurst proceeded to GODSTONE for duty and details to report to O.C. 45th Provisional Batt. MARGATE.	

Army Form C. 2118.

WAR DIARY
or
INTELLIGENCE SUMMARY.
(Erase heading not required.)

Instructions regarding War Diaries and Intelligence Summaries are contained in F. S. Regs., Part II. and the Staff Manual respectively. Title pages will be prepared in manuscript.

Hour, Date, Place	Summary of Events and Information	Remarks and References to Appendices
9.30 a.m. 1st October 1915. CROWBOROUGH.	A.D.S.T. Central Force inspected Divisional Supply Office at the Aines and proceeded to the Supply Depôt at Crowborough Goods Station and inspected books &c.	
4 p.m. 1st October 1915. MAIDSTONE.	Inspection by A.D.S.T. Central Force of Supply Depôt, Staff and Books.	
4 p.m. 12th October 1915. MAIDSTONE.	Supply Depôt 198th Infantry Brigade moved from Agricultural Hall to Monkton Drill Hall.	
10 a.m. 17th October 1915 TUNBRIDGE WELLS	Supply Details, 197th Infantry Brigade proceeded to TUNBRIDGE WELLS and took over Supply Duties. Depôt handed over by the Supplies 200th Infantry Brigade.	
10 a.m. 17th October 1915. TUNBRIDGE WELLS	First issue made from TUNBRIDGE WELLS Depôt to 197th Infantry Brigade.	

(9 29 6) W 2794 103,000 8/14 H W V Forms/C. 2118/11.

Army Form C. 2118.

WAR DIARY
or
INTELLIGENCE SUMMARY.
(Erase heading not required.)

Instructions regarding War Diaries and Intelligence Summaries are contained in F. S. Regs., Part II. and the Staff Manual respectively. Title pages will be prepared in manuscript.

Hour, Date, Place	Summary of Events and Information	Remarks and References to Appendices
0 a.m. 27.9.15. CROWBOROUGH.	Details of 2/1 South Eastern Mounted Brigade supplied with rations from Crowborough Depot.	
0 p.m. 28.9.15. MARESFIELD PARK	2/1 (Q.O.) Dorset Yeomanry attached to Division for Rations.	

T.B. Ayle, Major,
Senior Supply Officer,
66th (East Lancs.) Division.

Army Form C. 2118.

WAR DIARY
or
INTELLIGENCE SUMMARY.
(Erase heading not required.)

Instructions regarding War Diaries and Intelligence Summaries are contained in F. S. Regs., Part II. and the Staff Manual respectively. Title pages will be prepared in manuscript.

Hour, Date, Place	Summary of Events and Information	Remarks and References to Appendices
pm. 22nd October 1915. TUNBRIDGE WELLS	Complete issues made to units of Middlesex Infantry Brigade en route from Felmer Camp to Sevenoaks	
10 a.m. 25th October 1915. MAIDSTONE.	Supply Depot, Monkton Drill Hall, handed over to 67th (West Lancs.) Division. Supply details proceeded to CROWBOROUGH.	
28th & 29th October 1915. TUNBRIDGE.	Supplies issued to Advance Parties of battalions of 198th Infantry Brigade proceeding from BURHAM CAMP to CROWBOROUGH. by the supplies 197th Infantry Brigade.	

"The Limes"
Station Road
Crowborough.
1st November 1915.

T. B. Doyle. Major,
Senior Supply Officer,
66th (East Lancs.) Division.

Army Form C. 2118.

WAR DIARY
or
INTELLIGENCE SUMMARY.
(Erase heading not required.)

Instructions regarding War Diaries and Intelligence Summaries are contained in F. S. Regs., Part II, and the Staff Manual respectively. Title pages will be prepared in manuscript.

Hour, Date, Place	Summary of Events and Information	Remarks and References to Appendices
10 a.m., 1st October, 1915. CROWBOROUGH.	A.D.S.T. Central Force inspects Divisional Supply Office at the duties and proceeded to the Supply Depot at Crowborough Goods Station and inspected books etc.	
4 p.m. 1st October 1915. MAIDSTONE.	Inspection by A.D.S.T. Central Force of Supply Depot, Staff and Books.	
4 p.m. 12th October 1915. MAIDSTONE.	Supply Depot 198th Infantry Brigade moved from Agricultural Hall to Monkton Drill Hall.	
10 a.m. 17th October, 1915 TUNBRIDGE WELLS	Supply Details, 197th Infantry Brigade proceeded to TUNBRIDGE WELLS and took over Supply Duties. Depôt handed over by 0/c Supplies 200th Infantry Brigade.	
10 a.m. 19th October 1915. TUNBRIDGE WELLS	First issue made from TUNBRIDGE WELLS Depôt to 197th Infantry Brigade.	

Army Form C. 2118.

WAR DIARY
or
INTELLIGENCE SUMMARY.
(Erase heading not required.)

880. 16th Dec

Instructions regarding War Diaries and Intelligence Summaries are contained in F.S. Regs., Part II. and the Staff Manual respectively. Title pages will be prepared in manuscript.

Hour, Date, Place		Summary of Events and Information	Remarks and references to Appendices
10 a.m. 2nd November 1915. EAST GRINSTEAD.	3	Supply Depôt, EAST GRINSTEAD inspected by the Chief Inspector of Q.M.G. Services. No criticism. T.B.L.	
4 p.m. 2nd November 1915. CROWBOROUGH.	4	Divisional Supply Office inspected by C.I.Q.M.G Services. No criticism but various suggestions made by that Officer now being carried out. T.B.L.	
10 a.m. 3rd November 1915 CROWBOROUGH	5	Supply Depôt inspected by C.I.Q.M.G. Services. Suggestions made as to simpler mode of accounting for reduced ration as set out in Ind Army Order dated 7th August 1915. The suggestions are now being carried out with good results. T.B.L.	
3 p.m. 3rd November. 1915. TUNBRIDGE WELLS	7	Supply Depôt inspected by C.I.Q.M.G. Services. No criticism except that the bread was not well enough baked. The contractor has now been changed and the bread is of excellent quality. T.B.L.	

The Lewes
(Crowborough
2 XII. 15.

T.B. Lyle Major.
Senior Supply Officer.
66th (East Lancs) Division.

Army Form C. 2118.

WAR DIARY
or
INTELLIGENCE SUMMARY.
(Erase heading not required.)

Instructions regarding War Diaries and Intelligence Summaries are contained in F. S. Regs., Part II. and the Staff Manual respectively. Title pages will be prepared in manuscript.

Hour, Date, Place	Summary of Events and Information	Remarks and References to Appendices
pm. 22nd October 1915. NBRIDGE WELLS	Complete issues made to units of Middlesex Infantry Brigade en route from Falmer Camp to Sevenoaks	
0 a.m. 25th October 1915. IDSTONE.	Supply Depôt Moulton Drill Hall handed over to 67th (West Lancs) Division. Supply details provided to CROWBOROUGH.	
6th & 29th October 1915 NBRIDGE.	Supplies issued to Advance Parties of battalions of 198th Infantry Brigade proceeding from BURHAM CAMP to CROWBOROUGH, by the supplies 197th Infantry Brigade. TUNBRIDGE WELLS.	

"The Annis"
Station Road
Crowborough.
1st November 1915.

T. B. Doyle. Major,
Senior Supply Officer,
66th (East Lancs.) Division.

Army Form C. 2118.

WAR DIARY
or
INTELLIGENCE SUMMARY.
(Erase heading not required.)

Instructions regarding War Diaries and Intelligence
Summaries are contained in F.S. Regs., Part II.
and the Staff Manual respectively. Title pages
will be prepared in manuscript.

Hour, Date, Place	Summary of Events and Information	Remarks and references to Appendices
6pm 4th December 1915. EAST GRINSTEAD.	Supply duties at EAST GRINSTEAD handed over by Capt. G.P. Taylor to Lieut A. Clarke. T.B.L.	
10am 4th December 1915 CROWBOROUGH	Lieut R.M. Simpson, 4 N.C.Os and 3 men proceeded to ST. LEONARDS to take over supply duties from 67th (Home Counties) Divisional Train. T.B.L.	
4th December 1915 ST LEONARDS. HASTINGS	Depot at BEXHILL ROAD, ST LEONARDS handed over by 67th (Home Counties) Divisional Train, first issue made 10am 6th December. T.B.L.	
4 December 1915. EAST GRINSTEAD	34 (E Lancs) Howitzer Battery and 1/2nd Lancs Heavy Battery last rationed on moving to Maresfield Park UCKFIELD. T.B.L.	
7pm 9th December 1915 CROWBOROUGH.	37th Field Bakery, A.S.C. arrived from WAREHAM. Strength - 1 Officer (Lt. & Q.Mr. A.T. Bryan A.S.C.) 1 W.O. 91 other ranks. T.B.L.	
9 December 1915. CROWBOROUGH	Three bakers from 37th Field Bakery detached to Contractors for Bakery Bread for duty. Bakers drawn from Infantry Battalions returned to duty. T.B.L.	
Crowborough 31. XII. 15		T.B. Lyle. Major Senior Supply Officer 66th Divisional Train

Army Form C. 2118.

S.S.O. 16th Div.

WAR DIARY
or
INTELLIGENCE SUMMARY.
(Erase heading not required.)

Instructions regarding War Diaries and Intelligence Summaries are contained in F.S. Regs., Part II. and the Staff Manual respectively. Title pages will be prepared in manuscript.

Hour, Date, Place	Summary of Events and Information	Remarks and references to Appendices
3pm. 2nd November 1915. EAST GRINSTEAD.	Supply Depôt, EAST GRINSTEAD inspected by the Chief Inspector of Q.M.G. Services. No criticism. T.B.L.	
5pm. 2nd November 1915. CROWBOROUGH.	Divisional Supply Office inspected by C.I.Q.M.G. Services. No criticism but various suggestions made by that Officer now being carried out. T.B.L.	
10 a.m. 3rd November 1915 CROWBOROUGH	Supply Depôt inspected by C.I.Q.M.G. Services. Suggestions made as to simpler mode of accounting for reduced ration as set out in IInd Army Order dated 7th August 1915. The suggestions are now being carried out with good results. T.B.L.	
3pm. 3rd November. 1915. TUNBRIDGE WELLS	Supply Depôt inspected by C.I.Q.M.G. Service. No criticism except that the bread was not well enough baked. The contractor has now been changed and the bread is of excellent quality. T.B.L.	

The Lines
Crowborough
2.xii.15.

T.B. Lyle Major.
Senior Supply Officer.
66th (East Lancs) Division.

Forms/C. 2118/10

www.ingramcontent.com/pod-product-compliance
Lightning Source LLC
Chambersburg PA
CBHW081445160426
43193CB00013B/2391